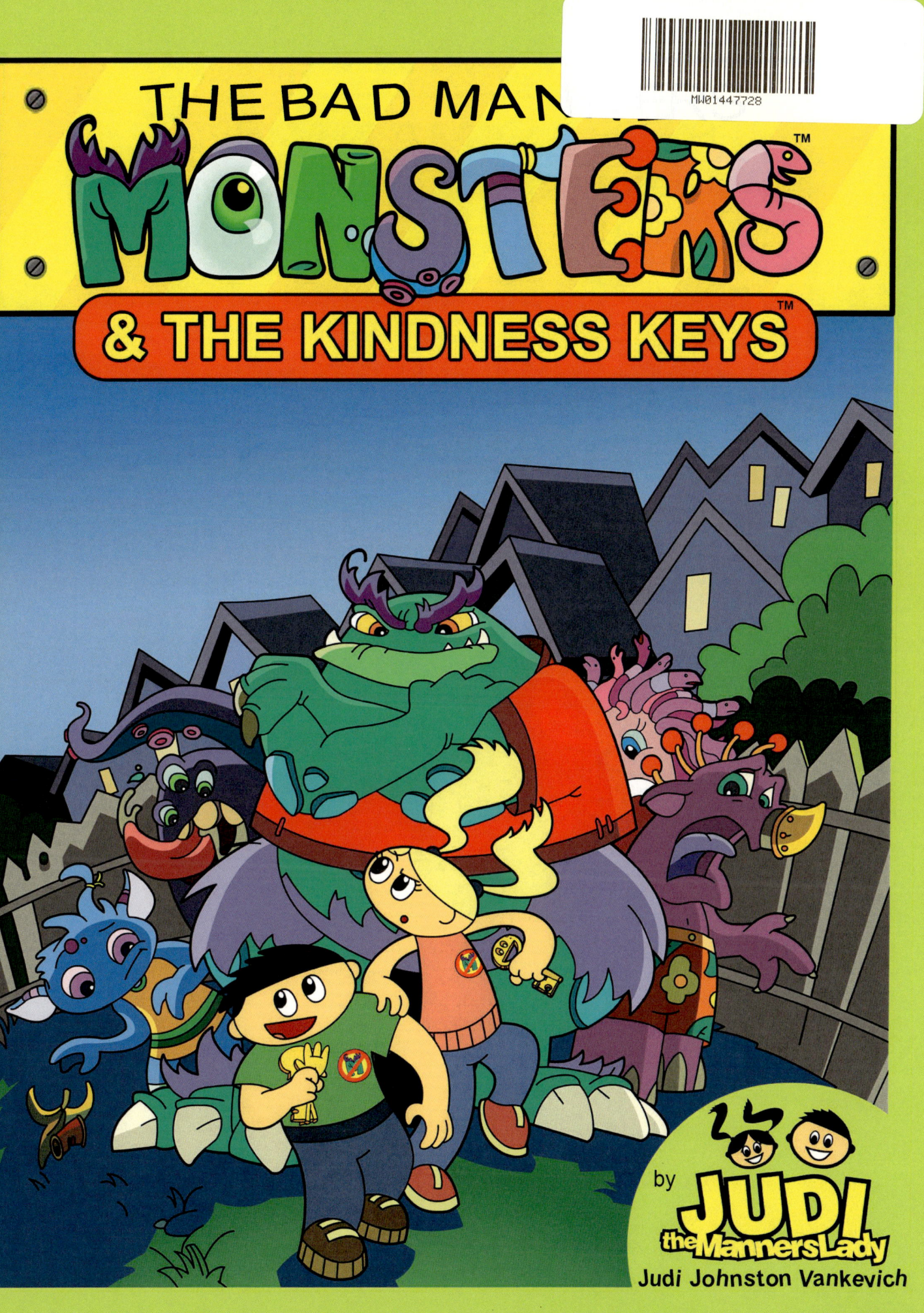

By Judi Johnston Vankevich
Art & Design by Dustan Windcliff

Dedicated with love to my children, Lexi, Zuri, and Sam; my husband, Ned; my grandchildren, Percy and Sophia Hudson; my parents, Margaret and Burt Johnston; Dustan's sons, David and Samuel Windcliff, and Dustan's wife, Eva.

ISBN: 978-1-959840-78-7
Copyright ©2023 Judi Vankevich
Manners Club Productions, A Division of The Manners Club & Life Skills International

Judi@TheMannersClub.com

All rights reserved. Written permission must be secured from the publisher to reproduce any part of this book, except for brief quotations in printed reviews.

**Dedicated to the children of today —
the leaders of tomorrow.**

Hey Kids, we're counting on you to have the courage to stop the Bad Manners Monsters from invading our families and our community.

Hold on tightly to your three Kindness Keys--the Kind Attitude Key, the Kind Words Key, and the Kind Actions Key! You will need them every day to capture and lock up the Bad Manners Monsters. We're proud of you as you go on this adventure.

Sincerely, *Judi!*

Judi The Manners Lady
Judi@TheMannersClub.com

Judi Johnston Vankevich is an award-winning singer, author, speaker, and educator, known and loved as Judi The Manners Lady.™ As President of the Manners Club & Life Skills International and Founder of the non-profit Civility Project, Judi is inspiring a new generation of young people to become strong young citizens who live with character, kindness, integrity, and gratitude. www.TheMannersLady.com

Dustan Windcliff is a Canadian artist who has worked on many animated TV productions and illustration projects. With his creative gifts, he captures the imagination of both adults and children alike.

www.TheMannersClub.com
www.BadMannersMonsters.com

THE KEYS FOR KINDNESS

It was a dangerous job but somebody had to do it.

Zack and Zoe, professional Bad Manners Busters, were on a new case. They looked around the town.

"Oh no!" cried Zoe. "They're here."

"Time for action," said Zack.

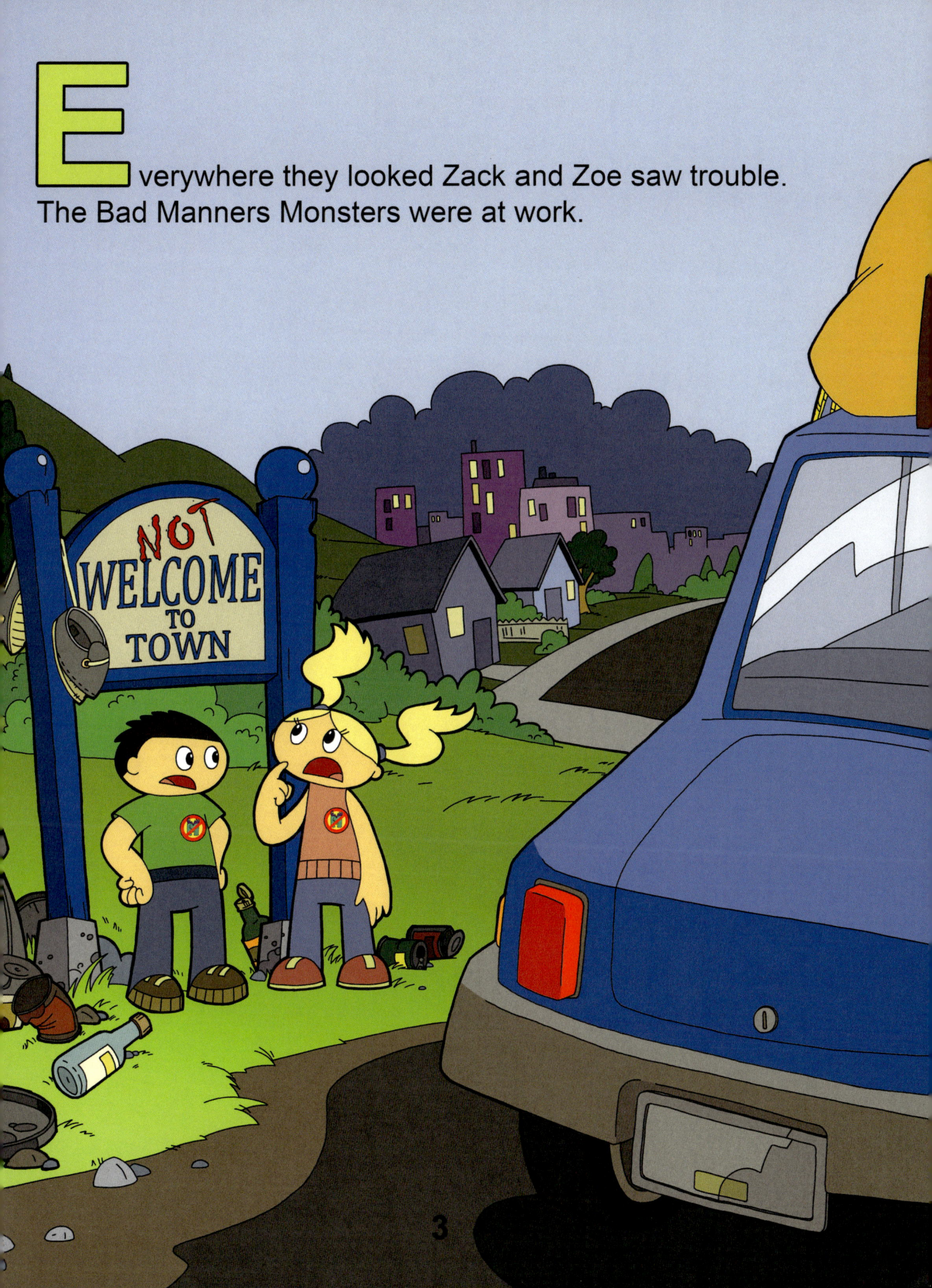

Everywhere they looked Zack and Zoe saw trouble. The Bad Manners Monsters were at work.

"Look!" Zoe exclaimed. "That little girl is whining. What a bad temper she has! Whiney-Rhino must be here somewhere."

Zoe was right. Just then, Whiney-Rhino, who always whined and complained, poked his head out from under the slide.

"**Z**oe, look!" said Zack. "That girl just littered!"

"Oh no!" replied Zoe. "Messy-Bessy is here too! Her bad influence is everywhere."

Zack and Zoe turned the corner.

"Gross!" exclaimed Zoe. "Do you see that kid chewing with his mouth open? Slobbo-Roo is at work!"

"Hey! What's going on at that school?" cried Zoe. "Those kids are completely out of control."

"It's Wiggly-Jiggly for sure!" said Zack. "Wiggly-Jiggly doesn't respect anyone. She's so disruptive."

Just then, Zack and Zoe saw a brother and sister fighting over a toy.

"Oh no!" groaned Zoe. "Grabba-Jabba is here! He loves it when people are greedy and selfish, and they take things that don't belong to them!"

"This town needs our help," said Zoe. "Why did they let the Bad Manners Monsters take over?"

"Let's go, Mom and Dad," said Zack. "It's time to bust the Bad Manners Monsters."

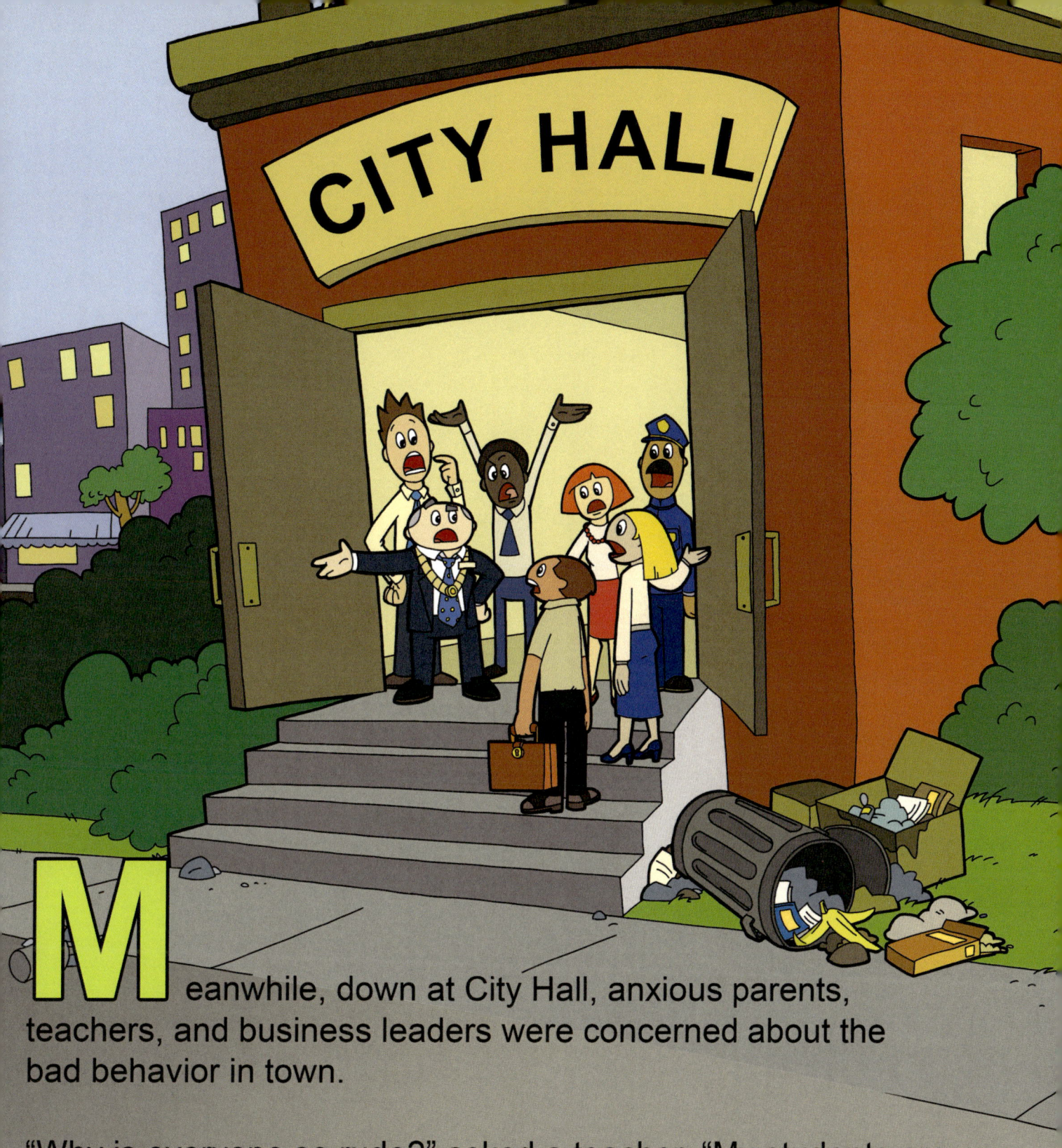

Meanwhile, down at City Hall, anxious parents, teachers, and business leaders were concerned about the bad behavior in town.

"Why is everyone so rude?" asked a teacher. "My students are always interrupting and not paying attention."

"Why are my children so messy and ungrateful?" asked a mother.

"Why is everyone so mean?" asked a little girl. "Our town isn't nice anymore!"

Zack and Zoe rushed into City Hall with their parents. "Excuse me, Mr. Mayor!" cried Zoe.

"Not now, kids," said the Mayor. "Our town is in big trouble!"

"We know!" exclaimed Zoe. "And we can help!"

"Who are you?" asked the Police Chief.

"We're the Bad Manners Busters," replied Zack. "We track the Bad Manners Monsters and help capture and lock them up."

"The Bad Manners Monsters?" asked the Police Chief.

13

"**Y**es, the Bad Manners Monsters," said Zoe. "They've invaded your town because people have forgotten to be kind."

"And if you don't catch them when they're little, they get bigger and stronger," added Zack. "That's why so many people have become grouchy, whiny, wiggly, grabby, slobby, and very messy."

Whiny-Rhino

Grouchy-Rouchy

Wiggly-Jiggly

Grabba-Jabba

Slobbo-Roo

Messy-Bessy

"This is terrible!" moaned the Mayor. "How do we get rid of them?"

"Our parents taught us there's only one way," said Zoe. "And it starts in the heart. A kind heart leads to kind attitudes, words, and actions. It's the secret to having good manners."

"I remember when we used to have good manners," said the Mayor. "Things were more civil back then, and people were more friendly."

"That's right," agreed the Police Chief. "So how do we capture these Bad Manners Monsters?"

"We have to use three golden keys to lock them up," said Zack.

"They're called the Kindness Keys," explained Zoe. "The Kind Attitude Key, the Kind Words Key, and the Kind Actions Key."

"And the Bad Manners Monsters can't stand them!" added Zack.

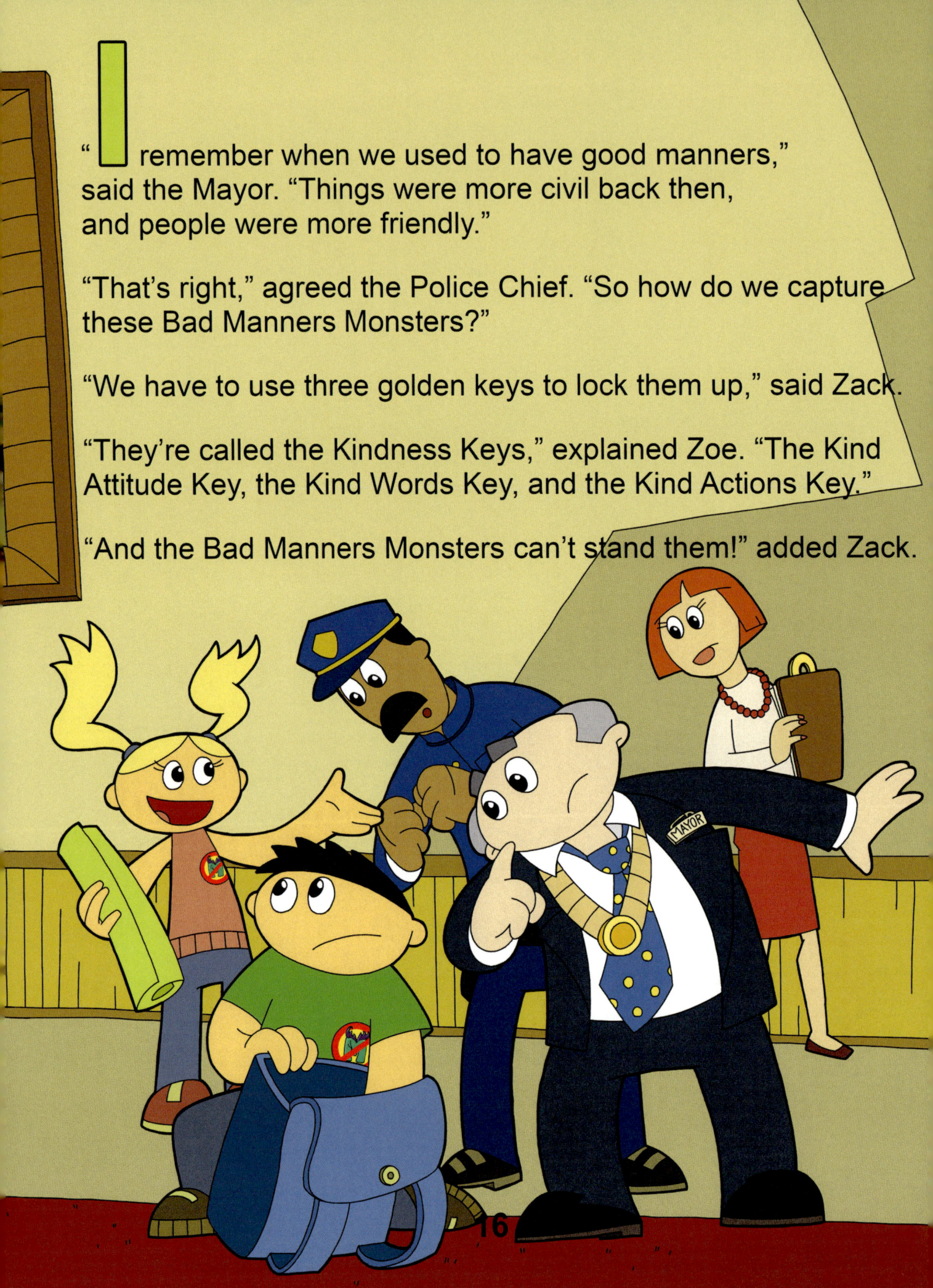

The Mayor smiled. "They remind me of the Golden Rule. Treat others the way you want to be treated."

"That's right!" said Zack. "And we'll show you how to use them to catch the Bad Manners Monsters."

#1 The Kind Attitude Key

"First, let's start with the Kind Attitude Key," said Zoe. "A good attitude makes the other keys work."

A teacher shared the Kind Attitude Keys with her students and soon they were more friendly and kind.

Suddenly, Grouchy-Rouchy leaped from behind a tree and growled, "NOOO! Not the Kindness Keys!"

Just then, a huge chain grabbed Grouchy-Rouchy, and a boy rushed over with his Kind Attitude Key and locked him up.

"We caught him!" cheered the kids as the Police Chief dragged Grouchy-Rouchy off to the town jail.

"Let's get the rest of the monsters," said the Mayor.

#2 The Kind Words Key

"The second key," explained Zack, "is the the Kind Words Key."

"You mean like 'Please' and 'Thank you'?" asked the Mayor.

"Precisely," said Zoe as she passed out the Kind Words Keys.

Soon children began to say, "Please," and "Thank you," when they asked for something, and parents and teachers replied, "You're welcome!"

Shoppers said, "Excuse me!" when they bumped into someone.

And people said, "I'm sorry. Will you forgive me?" when they did something wrong.

All their kind words made Whiney-Rhino explode. "Stop it!" he screamed. "No more kind words!"

Just then another chain grabbed Whiny-Rhino and the kids ran over with their Kind Words Keys to lock him up.

"Hurray!" everyone cheered as the Police Chief dragged Whiney-Rhino off to jail. "No more mean words!"

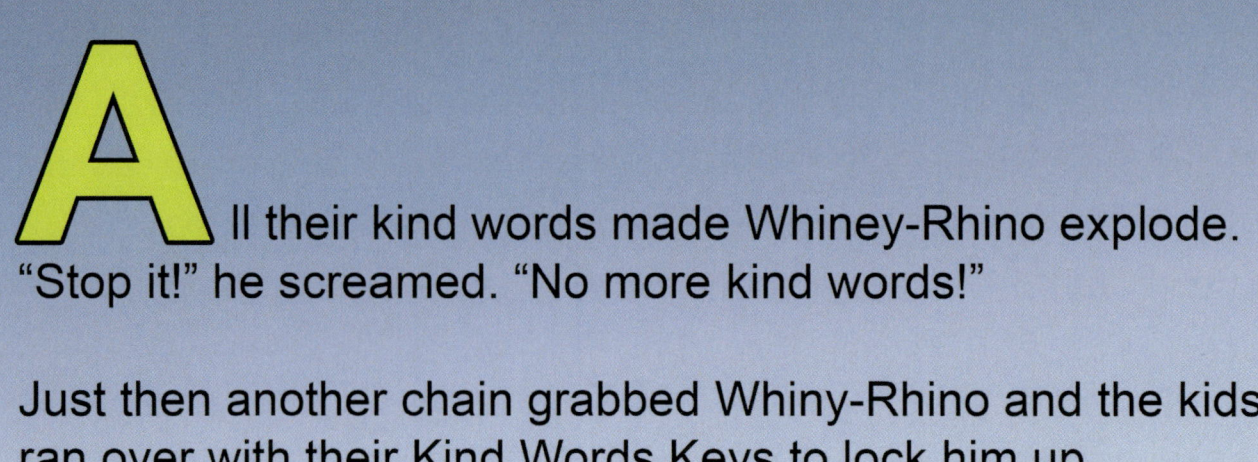

#3 The Kind Actions Key

"Good job, team!" congratulated Zack. "Now let's use the Kind Actions Key!"

As the Kind Actions Keys were passed around, brothers and sisters started sharing their toys, and neighbors greeted each other with a friendly smile.

At that moment, Grabba-Jabba flew through town in a fury. "Stop sharing!" he yelled. "No more being kind!"

But everyone ignored him. Frustrated, Grabba-Jabba tried to run away, but a chain grabbed him, and the kids eagerly locked him up with their Kind Actions Keys.

Soon everyone started cleaning up their town. They picked up litter, cleaned their messy bedrooms, and even washed the dirty dishes.

Just then, Messy-Bessy was swept out the door. "I don't like tidy rooms!" she cried, as a chain grabbed her, and the children quickly turned their Kind Actions Keys in her lock.

The town was becoming more pleasant. Even mealtimes were more fun, as children chewed their food politely, had good conversation, and even remembered to thank their parents for a delicious dinner.

Suddenly, Slobbo-Roo leaped up from under the table and roared, "No more good manners! I can't stand them!"

The children cheered as they locked him up with their Kind Actions Keys.

At school, the children used their Kind Actions Keys and became more respectful.

Wiggily-Jiggly was furious. She couldn't get the students to be disruptive anymore. Before she could run away, the children captured her and took her to jail with all the other Bad Manners Monsters.

The Bad Manners Monsters growled as they rattled their cage. Zack and Zoe counted the monsters. "One, two, three, four, five, six. Great job! We caught them all!"

"Hurray!" everyone cheered. "The Kindness Keys really work!"

"Well done, everyone," said the Mayor. "Good manners make good citizens and that makes our town safer."

"And more fun, too!" smiled a little girl.

Just then, the Bad Manners Monsters began to shrink. "Look! They're getting smaller!" exclaimed a parent.

"That's right," said Zoe. "The Kindness Keys drain the monsters of their power. But be careful. They are sneaky and will try to come back. So, remember to guard your heart and hang on to your Kindness Keys."

"Hurray for the Bad Manners Busters!" said the Police Chief. "Thank you for helping us capture and lock up the Bad Manners Monsters."

"You're welcome," replied Zoe. "And now with your Kindness Keys, you can be Bad Manners Busters, too!"

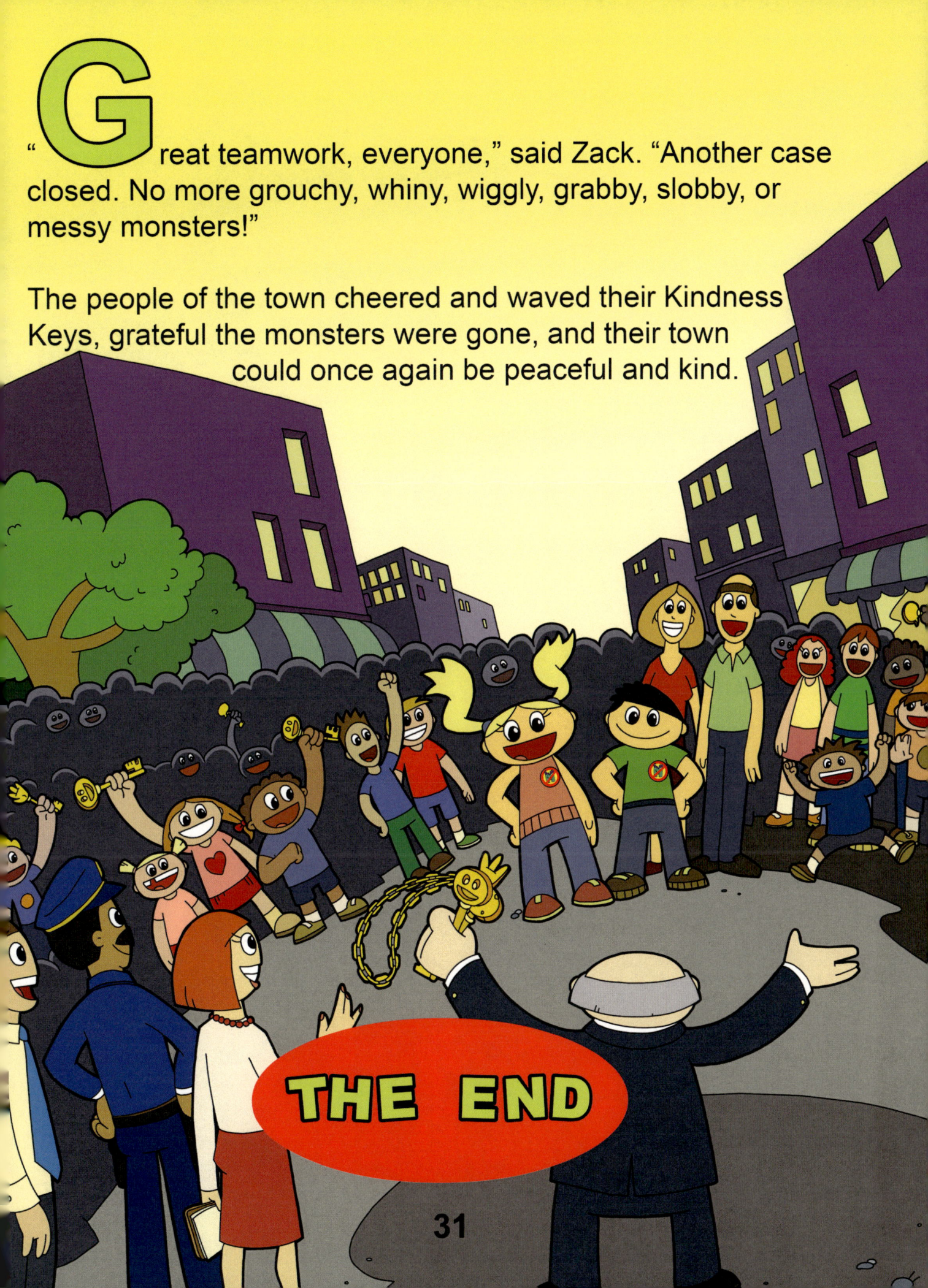

"**G**reat teamwork, everyone," said Zack. "Another case closed. No more grouchy, whiny, wiggly, grabby, slobby, or messy monsters!"

The people of the town cheered and waved their Kindness Keys, grateful the monsters were gone, and their town could once again be peaceful and kind.

THE END

Hey Kids!

The Kindness Keys really work! Use them to capture and lock up the Bad Manners Monsters whenever they try to sneak into your town, your home, or your heart.

Your friend,
Judi The Manners Lady

P.S. Download your Kindness Keys and official "The Bad Manners Buster" Badge at www.TheMannersClub.com

Sing the Bad Manners Monsters song along with Judi the Manners Lady.

by
JUDI The Manners Lady

FUZZY-WUZZY HEART

The Bad Manners Monsters are coming to town!
The Bad Manners Monsters are lurking around!
They're looking for someone with a bad attitude!
But don't be fooled! They'll only make you rude!

The GROUCHY-ROUCHY—he's not any fun!
The GROUCHY-ROUCHY—he makes all the kids run!
He's mean and he's nasty—but he ends up alone…
If he isn't nice, he'll always be on his own!

The GRABBA-JABBA—always wants to be first!
The GRABBA-JABBA—doesn't care who he hurts!
He grabs the biggest and he grabs the best,
But he'll always be lonely, this I must confess!

The MESSY-BESSY—never washes her hands!
The MESSY-BESSY—litters up the land!
Her room is so messy—and disorganized!
She can't find a thing! Well, I'm not surprised!

The WHINEY-RHINO—has a bad attitude!
The WHINEY-RHINO—is always so rude!
He never is thankful and he whines and complains—
But no one will like him if he's always a pain!

The WIGGLY-JIGGLY—always wiggles and squirms!
The WIGGLY-JIGGLY—never waits her turn!
She never sits still and interrupts everyone!
The WIGGLY-JIGGLY isn't any fun!

The SLOBBO-ROO—he always eats like a goop!
The SLOBBO-ROO—slurps up all of his soup!
He licks all his fingers as he gobbles his food!
But he eats all alone because he's always so rude!

The Bad Manners Monsters are coming to town!
The Bad Manners Monsters are lurking around!
They're looking for someone with a bad attitude!
But don't be fooled! They'll only make you rude!

So if the Bad Manners Monsters try to get in your way,
You tell the Bad Manners Monsters to "GO AWAY!"
You don't want to be mean and you don't want to be rude!
You want to be polite and have a great attitude!

GROUCHY-ROUCHY

WIGGLY-JIGGLY

GRABBA-JABBA

SLOBBO-ROO

MESSY-BESSY

WHINEY-RHINO

Download your free "Bad Manners Monsters" song and official "Bad Manners Buster" card at
www.TheMannersClub.com.

Made in the USA
Monee, IL
08 September 2023

41962583R10024